Designing for CINEMAS

Dear Reader

Like most people, I love going to cinemas to watch movies. I have often thought about the talented people who create these special places for us to enjoy movies with our families and friends.

So I decided to write a book about the people who design cinemas, to find out how they create a space for us to be entertained.

CHECK OUT CHAPTER NINE TO FIND OUT WHY DOGS ARE AT THE MOVIES, TOO!

My research led me to some very helpful people with a passion for movies and cinemas. One of these people is Ian Swan, an architect who specialises in designing cinemas. Join Ian, on pages 8–27, as he takes you on a tour inside one of his favourite cinemas.

Enjoy!

Sharon Parsons

My sincere thanks to the following people for their time, information, images and enthusiasm for this book:

Ian Swan, Brisbane, Australia
Terry Jackman and team at the Loganholme Hyperplex Cinemas, Brisbane, Australia
Frank Gibson, Brisbane, Australia
Graham Tienan, Brisbane, Australia
Richard Parton, Brisbane, Australia
David Kilderry, Lunar Drive-In, Melbourne, Australia
Moonlight Cinemas, Melbourne, Australia
Royal Botanic Gardens, Melbourne, Australia
Nikki Williams, Melbourne, Australia
Karen, Sam and Kate Rafferty, Melbourne, Australia

For learning solutions, visit cengage.com.au

Contents

Designing for CINEMAS

1 Shoosh, the Movie Has Started

Everyone loves to see movies at the cinema, but think about a time when there were only black-and-white movies with no sound – they were called silent movies. Entertainers used to perform music or narrate a story while the silent movie was screened, to add extra entertainment for the audience. Title cards on the screen told what was happening; the audience had to read fast before the next scene! Even in those pre-digital days, going to the cinema was an interactive experience.

images from the silent movie era

Talkies

From the late 1920s "talkies", or movies with sound, were produced. Today, technology has advanced so much that we can see movies in 2-D and 3-D on massive screens in multi-cinema complexes, at drive-in cinemas and in garden settings. We can also watch movies in planes, and on computers, mobile phones and other hand-held devices.

4-D MOVIES

This term refers to a special kind of movie experience – viewing 3-D movies in places like theme parks with extra physical effects, such as vibrating chairs, wind or special lighting.

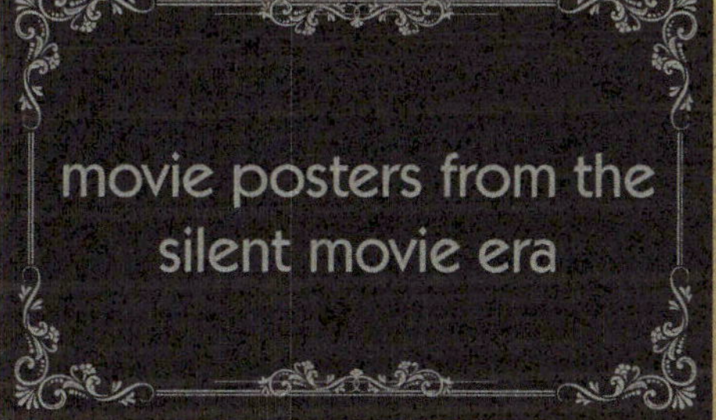
movie posters from the silent movie era

Charlie Chaplin, the actor

Charlie Chaplin, the director

A Great Silent Movie Actor

Charlie Chaplin (1889–1977) was born in England and he was a famous actor and director of silent movies. He created a vagrant character called "the tramp", who had nice manners and wore good-quality clothes. Charlie performed his tramp characterisation in many movies because it was so popular.

A Movie Timeline

1894

Black-and-white silent movies

early 1900s

Black-and-white silent movies + title cards

2

early 1900s

Black-and-white movies + sound

1920s

Colour movies + sound

1990s

Colour movies with more special effects

2000s

3-D movies more popular + digital movies

6

DIRECTOR

a movie poster for The Tramp

Every year, hundreds of new movies are released into cinemas worldwide. In 2010, almost 900 new movies made about 10 billion dollars at the box office. So how do movies get from studios to cinemas? Follow an example of a movie trail below.

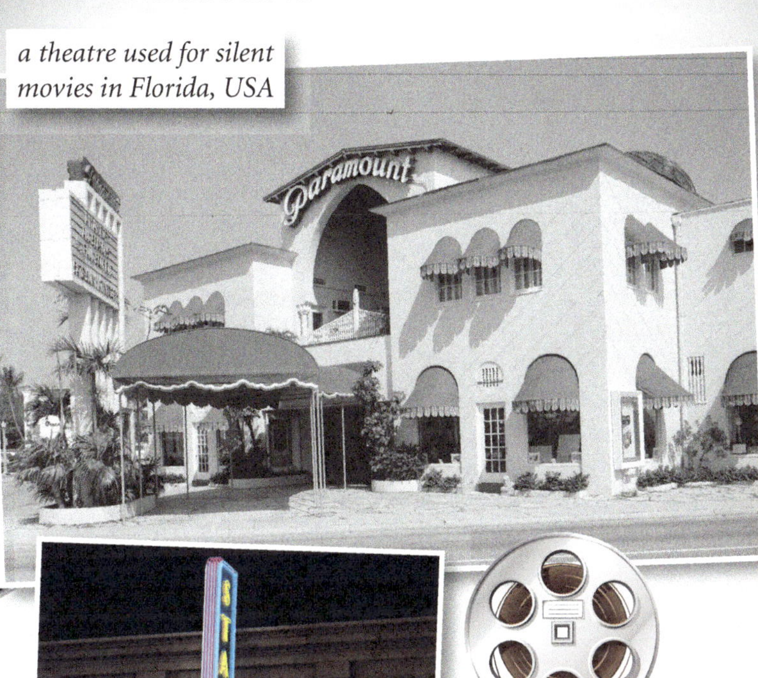

a theatre used for silent movies in Florida, USA

1. **Movie studio companies** (produce or make the movies)
2. **Film distribution companies** (make copies of the movies and hire them to the cinemas for a negotiated period of time)
3. **Exhibitors** (companies or individual people who manage cinemas)

TOP 5 MOST PROFITABLE MOVIES OF ALL TIME

In 2011, the movies that had made the most money ever were:

Avatar (2009): 2.8 billion dollars; ***Titanic*** (1997): 1.8 billion dollars; ***Lord of the Rings – Return of the King*** (2003): 1.1 billion dollars; ***Pirates of the Caribbean – Dead Man's Chest*** (2006): 1.1 billion dollars and ***Toy Story 3*** (2010): 1.1 billion dollars.

2 Who Designs Cinemas?

Architect, Ian Swan

Ian Swan is an Australian architect who has specialised in designing cinema interiors for about 30 years. When he began designing cinemas, they were stand-alone cinemas for 35-mm film movies, whereas today they are multiplex cinemas for 2-D and 3-D movies, with 35-mm film projectors and digital projectors, in large shopping centres.

Most cinemas are built inside or adjacent to shopping centres. Ian needs to know what kind of cinema shell has been built for him to work with. The three kinds of cinema shells are:

Cold-Water Shell: the shopping centre owner only builds the roof, and the internal and external walls.

Warm-Water Shell: the shopping centre owner builds a cold-water shell but pays for electrical wiring, air conditioning and heating.

Hot-Water Shell: the shopping centre owner will pay for everything attached to the cinema shell. In these cases, a movie exhibition company asks an architect like Ian to design the lighting and sound systems, fittings (e.g. seats and carpets) and special areas (e.g. the projection room).

Ian Swan inside a cinema that he designed at the Loganholme multiplex

THE MOST REWARDING PART OF MY JOB IS WHEN I SEE PEOPLE ENJOYING MY CINEMA DESIGNS.
IAN SWAN

A 12-Cinema Multiplex

Ian Swan is most proud of a 12-cinema multiplex that he designed in Loganholme, Brisbane, Australia. Fifteen years ago, it started out as an eight-cinema multiplex, but as demand increased, four more cinemas were designed and built. Ian Swan takes pride in designing unique-looking cinemas where people can enjoy special movie experiences.

> “MULTIPLEXES OFFER CHOICE FOR CONSUMERS.”
>
> RICHARD PARTON, CINEMA MANAGER

3 Cinema Design and Layout

From **Brief** to **Drawings**

Before Ian can start work on the design and layout, he discusses the cinema brief with the cinema owner. After their initial series of meetings, Ian can start creating some drawings and layouts for the cinema owner's comment and approval. Then Ian can prepare final drawings for council approval.

A Cinema Brief

The brief for a new cinema multiplex will feature a range of requirements that the architect must include in the drawings and design. An example is outlined below.

A New Cinema Brief

Architectural Style: Art Deco

Artwork: large Art Deco and movie inspired artwork

Colour Palette: bright, fresh colours to suit the "Sunshine State" location in Queensland, Australia

Projection Room: for six digital and six 35-mm film projectors and equipment

Carpets: original Art Deco inspired design for each cinema

Twelve Stadium-Style Cinemas

- Three 400-seat cinemas*
- Three 320-seat cinemas**
- Two 250-seat cinemas**
- Two 150-seat cinemas**
- Two Star cinemas (82-seats and 62-seats)**

*20-metre-wide by 9-metre-high screens

**18-metre-wide by 9-metre-high screens

Seats and **Steps**

One of Ian's first jobs is to decide on the best seat design and seating layout to suit the size and theme of each cinema. His main objectives are to ensure that people are comfortable and their "sight lines" are good from any seat.

Dark-coloured and durable upholstery is important.

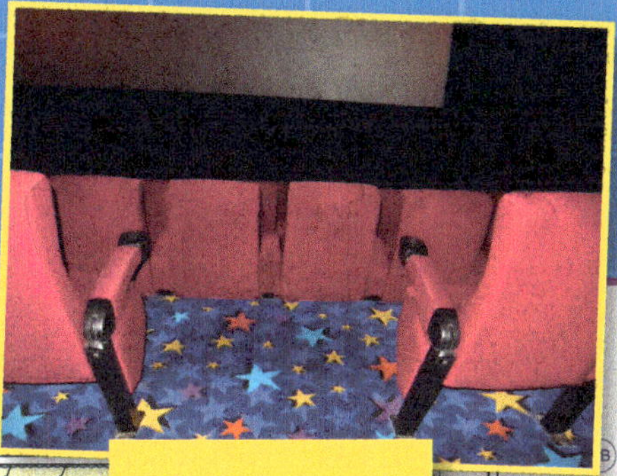

wheelchair access

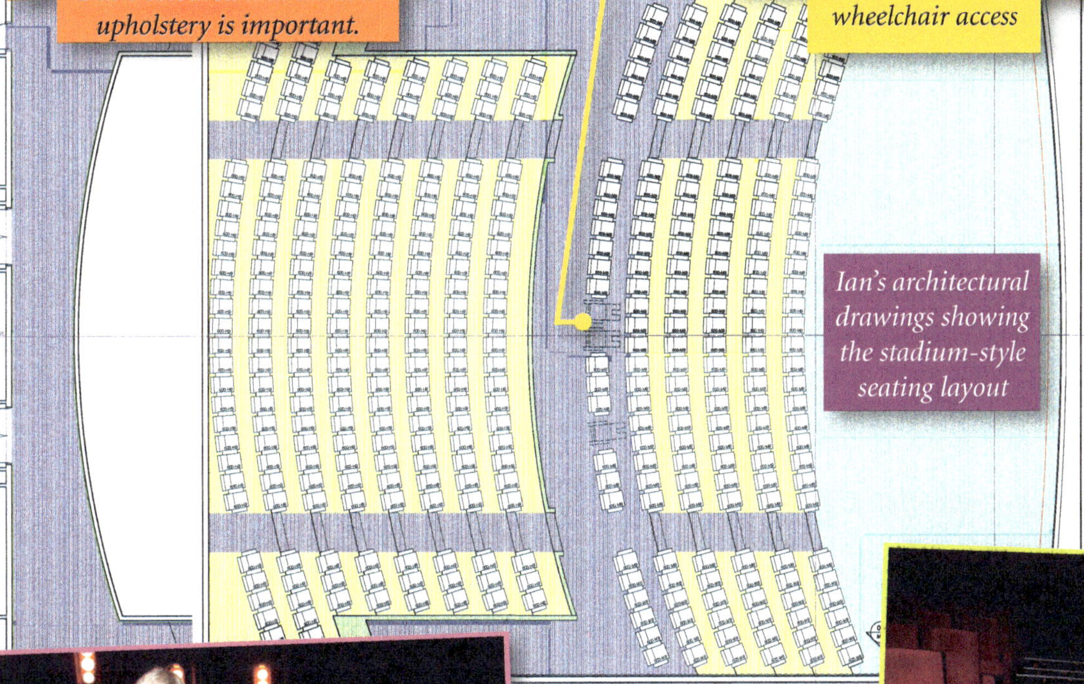

Ian's architectural drawings showing the stadium-style seating layout

Ian checks the lift-up arm rests between the high-backed "couple" seats.

Steps with rubber strips and seat lights provide extra safety.

Screens and Speakers

Look Up at the Screens

Ian designs the biggest screen he can fit into the available cinema space.

Films are screened in two main formats – wide-screen and cinemascope – so Ian has to design two side-masking screens (2.7 metres wide).

The movable masking screens slide inwards slightly when a wide-screen movie has finished. Then the projectionist is ready to show a cinemascope movie on the narrower screen.

Ian's drawings show the movable masking screens on both sides of the cinemascope screen.

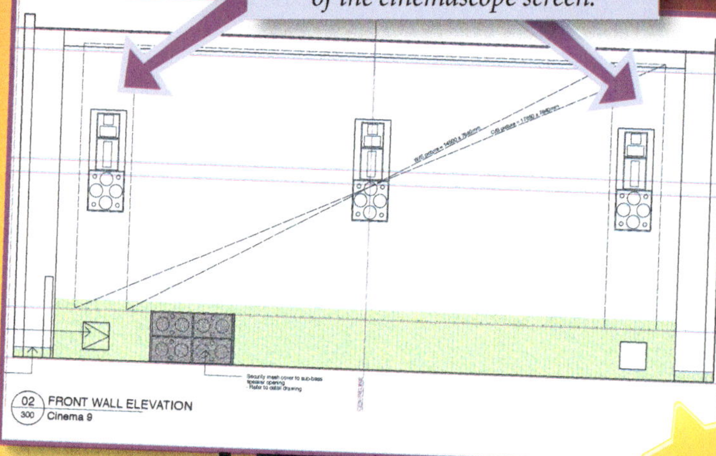

Listen to the Speakers

Multiple speakers provide surround sound. Ian's drawings show the exact positions of the different speakers.

Ian's drawings also show the speakers that are arranged on every wall of the cinema.

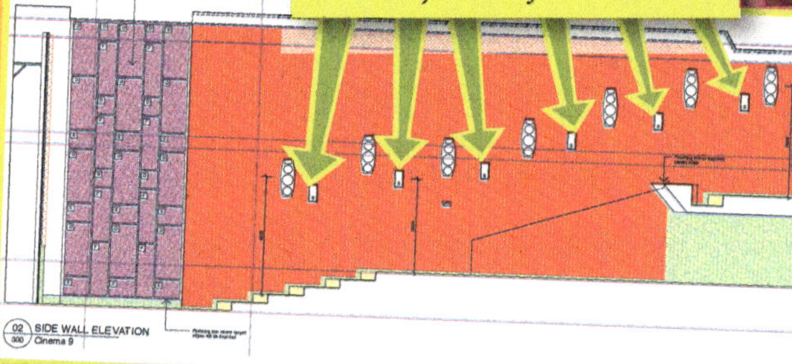

Wall speakers are covered in acoustic fabric to absorb the sound.

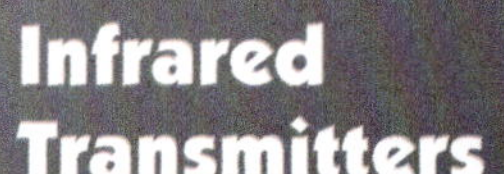

Infrared Transmitters

Infrared transmitters send the movie soundtrack to headphones worn by people with hearing impairments.

Safety and Signs

Ian's drawings include all the safety features required by the building codes and regulations of the Queensland and Australian governments.

Safety Rails

Fire Safety Point

Illuminated Exit Signs

Ramp Access

Carpets, Curtains and Colour

Original Carpet Designs

Ian uses a digital design program to create the new carpet patterns so that they can be approved by the cinema owner before the carpets are manufactured. Patterned carpets with dark colours work best because they do not show stains if people spill drinks and food. The most common carpet colours are maroon and dark blue. The carpet has to be woven with the strongest synthetic pile to withstand heavy and constant foot traffic.

Durable and Colourful Carpets

Acoustic Fabric Curtains

Colour everywhere!

Services Galore!

Customer Services

All cinemas must provide patrons with standard services and facilities, according to public building regulations. Ian ensures that these facilities are designed to suit the overall theme of the cinema.

> IT'S A JUGGLING ACT TO FIT IT ALL IN.
>
> IAN SWAN

Foyer Services

Easy-to-Read Signs

Rubbish Bins

3-D Glasses Bins

Male Toilets

Female Toilets

4 Inside the Projection Room

Movies on **Film** and **Disks**

The projection room at a cinema multiplex has to accommodate the large 35-mm film projectors and the smaller digital projectors. When Ian designs a projection room, he makes sure the room is big enough to allow sufficient air to flow around these hot machines.

Digital projectors produce a lot of heat, so Ian checks that the vent system is working well.

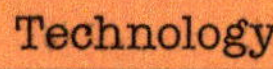

Advantages and Disadvantages of Digital Disk Distribution

New digital movie disks provide advantages for film distribution companies because they are quicker and less expensive to produce. The disks are smaller and lighter than 35-mm reels of film, so they are also cheaper to post to the cinemas around the country.

The disadvantage for the cinema multiplexes is that screening date codes are embedded in each disk. Once the screening date codes have expired, the disk cannot be used again. When a movie is more popular than the cinema operators originally thought, they have to buy more time in the form of another screening code from the film distributor. With 35-mm film reels, they can show the movie many times for as long as enough people want to see the movie.

a digital disk stacker

a film platter

Extremely Hot Xenon Bulbs

Movie projectors use a complex series of parts and processes to project the images onto the screen. They require a powerful light source in the form of a xenon bulb (lamp) mounted to the centre of a parabolic mirror inside the projector's lamphouse. The mirror reflects extreme focussed heat (about 850 degrees Celsius) so Ian must design excellent ventilation systems.

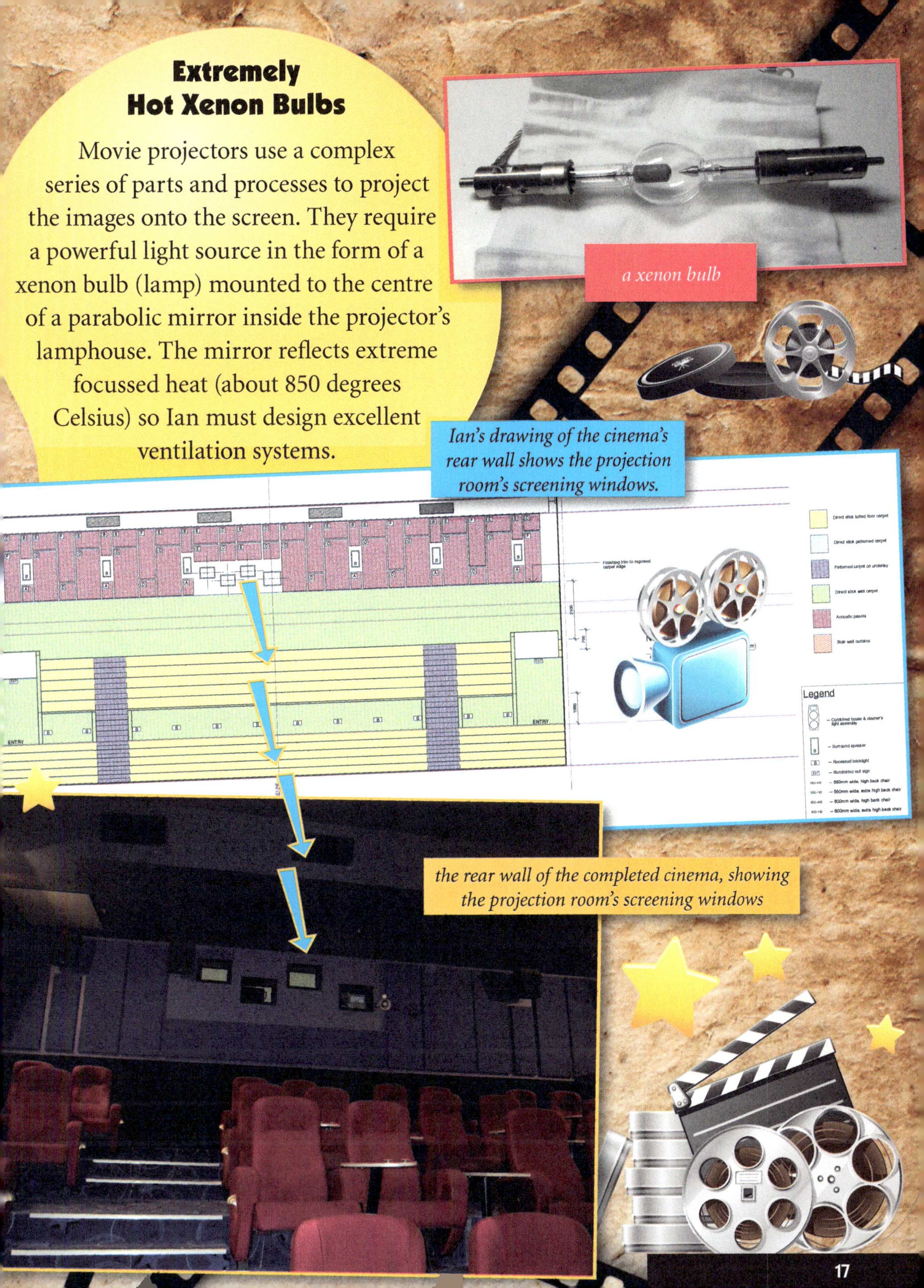

a xenon bulb

Ian's drawing of the cinema's rear wall shows the projection room's screening windows.

the rear wall of the completed cinema, showing the projection room's screening windows

Frank, a Movie Projectionist

Frank Gibson has worked as a movie projectionist for over 50 years and he has been the Head Projectionist at the Loganholme cinema multiplex for 22 years. Frank operates 12 projectors – six film and six digital – in a large projection room. Frank has to move quickly between projectors so sometimes he rides his scooter!

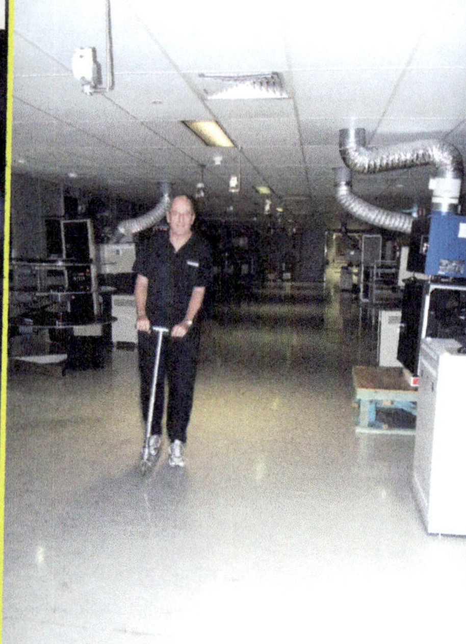

The projection room has enough space for Frank to move around safely, even on his scooter.

Film Splicing

Most movies are still provided to cinema projectionists on 35-mm film reels by film distribution companies. Several reels are usually needed for one movie. These reels need to be joined together, or spliced, and placed on large film platters.

Frank joins up the movie's reels and then splices in the trailers for new movies and advertisements.

> FILM FOR THE MOVIE *TITANIC* (1997) WAS ON TEN REELS (115 METRES LONG)! MOST MOVIES ARE ON ABOUT FIVE TO SEVEN REELS OF FILM.
>
> FRANK GIBSON

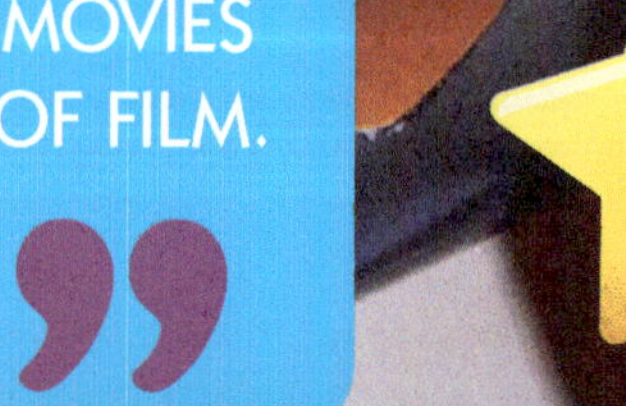

Threading Film to the Projector

Once the large, heavy reel of film is on the platter, the film is threaded to the film projector in a complex configuration.

Screening Schedule

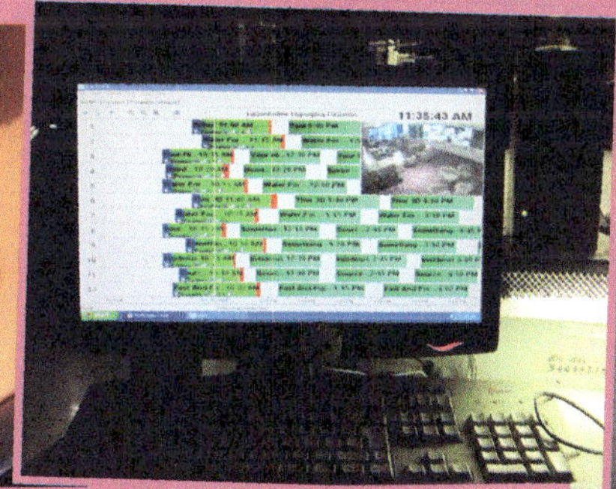

Frank checks the movie screening schedule for the day.

Lights, Sound and Screen System

The Pennywise computer system has been programmed to operate the lights, sound systems and the movie projectors at the right times.

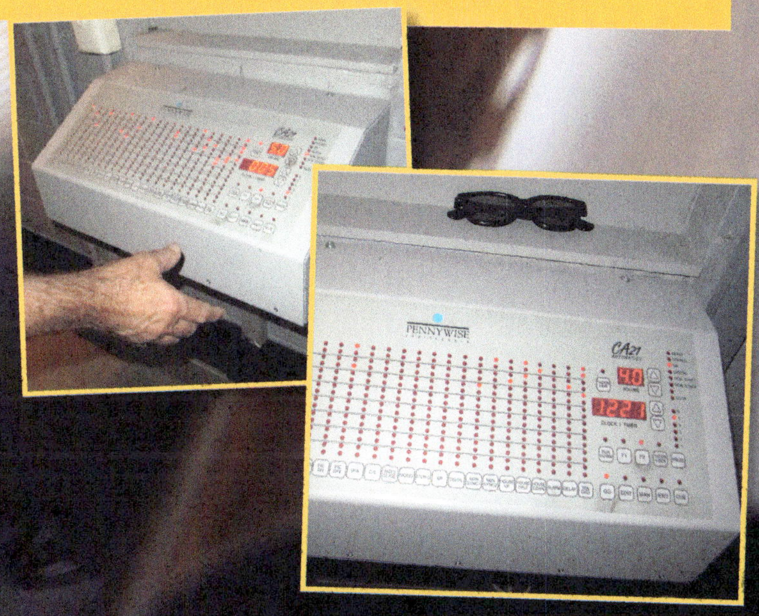

5 Welcome to the Cinema!

Enter to Get Your **Ticket!**

Ian Swan has designed an inviting entrance, foyer and ticket office to make people feel relaxed and excited about coming to the cinema.

a meeting place outside

an inviting entrance

A sales assistant is ready to help with tickets.

a friendly ticket collector

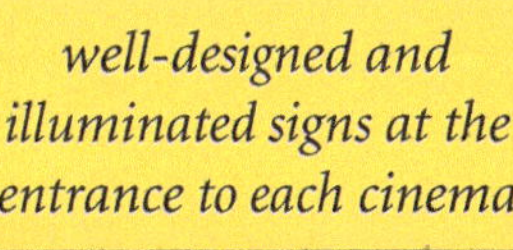

well-designed and illuminated signs at the entrance to each cinema

Cinema administration provides support for cinema staff and movie patrons.

Making Popcorn at the Cinema

Popcorn is Tops!

Goal

To make popcorn at the cinema.

Materials

1. A popcorn machine that is large enough to cater for many customers.
2. A large bag of popping corn kernels tossed in oil and salt.

Anyone for popcorn?

Technology

How Does the Popcorn Kettle Work?

The stainless steel kettle is suspended from the top of the popcorn machine. It heats up the starch inside the corn kernels at a temperature of about 250 degrees Celsius. Good-quality corn kernels have enough moisture to create light, fluffy popcorn. The moisture and the hot starch inside the kernels swell so much that the outer shells burst and white, fluffy popped corn pops out. In minutes, the sound of corn popping can be heard. The pressure of the corn popping inside the kettle causes the lid to lift and pushes the popcorn into the warm glass cavity.

Steps

1. Turn on the kettle switch, the light switch and the warmer tray switch.

2. When the kettle has warmed up to about 250 degrees Celsius, tip the corn kernels into the kettle.

3. After three to four minutes, listen for the sound of the corn starting to pop, and watch for the kettle's lid beginning to lift from the pressure of the popping corn.

4. Open the glass doors and use the kettle's handle to tip out all of the popped corn onto the warming tray below.

5. Use the popcorn scoop to move the popcorn evenly over the warming tray. The corn that did not pop will fall through the tray's tiny holes into a dispenser below.

Ready to Serve

TECHNOLOGY FEATURE

Who Invented the Popcorn Machine?

American inventor Charles Cretors made the first popcorn machine in 1893 – it could roast peanuts as well as pop corn kernels. This early machine used steam to make the motor work, not electricity.

Today, the Cretors family continue to manufacture popcorn-making machines in Chicago, USA. Their largest popcorn machine can make 2260 kilograms of popcorn an hour!

an early Cretors' peanut and popcorn machine

a Cretors' peanut and popcorn wagon

Q & A

Q: Where is the world's only popcorn machine museum?

A: A large number of historic popcorn machines are in a museum in Marion, Ohio in the USA. Some of the best popping corn kernels are grown in Ohio.

Q: What is used to cook the popcorn?

A: Most machines use oil to cook the popcorn; some others use hot air.

Q: Is popcorn healthy?

A: Some of the nutrients in popping corn are carbohydrates, fibre and vitamins B1 and B2.

an early Cretors' advertisement

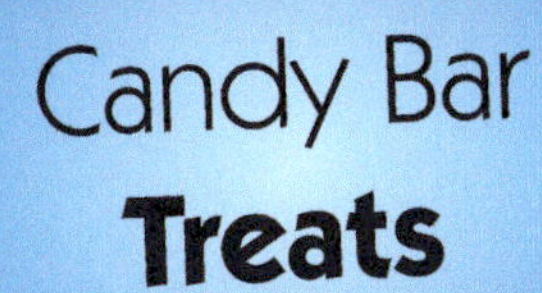

For most people, a cinema experience is not quite complete without a treat of some kind. The place to buy snacks at the cinema is called a candy bar – a term that originated in the USA.

Have we got enough to eat?

Designing the Candy Bar

Ian designs a candy bar that looks inviting and colourful, and allows people to access the area easily and quickly. Popcorn is the biggest seller at the candy bar, so Ian ensures that he designs enough space for the popcorn machines because they cannot afford to run out!

7 A Star Cinema

Everyone Is a **Star!**

Most cinemas offer their patrons an extra-special movie experience. For the Star Cinema, Ian Swan developed a unique luxury experience for patrons. He even created a carpet with a unique star-shaped design, just for this cinema.

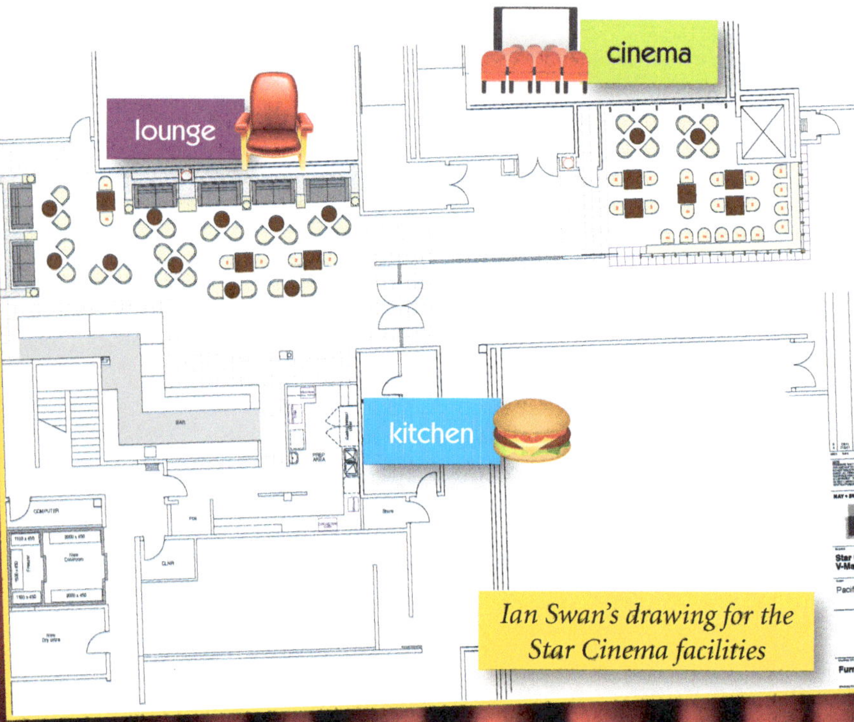

Ian Swan's drawing for the Star Cinema facilities

The Star Cinema

a welcoming and comfortable entrance at the Star Cinema

Sit in the Star Lounge

Ian designed comfortable and attractive lounges.

Be Seated

Ian chose extra plush seats.

What's on the Menu?

Ian made sure the kitchen was state-of-the-art.

Cleaning Up

Most of the time, cinema patrons are careful with their food and drinks. But cinema cleaners Lisa and Anna agree that the most common clean-up job involves vomit! The second most common problem for cleaners is sticky lollies squashed into the seats.

Lisa is ready to clean the Star Cinema.

Lisa and Anna work quickly, because another movie is about to begin.

Drive into Australia's Largest Drive-In

What name would you call a drive-in theatre? Well, Australia's largest drive-in theatre, also one of its oldest, is called the Lunar Drive-In. It is a good name because the word "lunar" is used when referring to the Moon.

In Roman mythology, Luna is the goddess of the Moon.

1956 – Drive-In Opens

The Lunar Drive-In was opened in 1956, which was before television was available in Australia. It had only one wooden screen and enough space for 650 cars. In those days, a driver would park their car beside a steel speaker post and put the speaker inside their car.

Today, people tune their car radio into an FM station to hear the movie's soundtrack.

The sun sets on the drive-in.

1980s – Drive-Ins Close

In the 1980s, Video Cassette Recorders (VCRs) became popular, so more people watched movies at home and stopped going to drive-ins. Many drive-ins closed, including the Lunar Drive-In.

watching a video via a VCR

2002 – Drive-In Reopens

In 2002, the Lunar Drive-In reopened with two massive new steel screens. A third screen was added in 2003. Many families with young children go to early evening movies, and everyone enjoys snuggling into their pillows and doonas with a big box of popcorn!

the new cafe

Bring Your Pooch to the Movies!

Moonlight Cinemas provide outdoor movie experiences in city gardens around Australia. In 2008, each garden cinema offered dog owners the chance to take their dogs to the movie premiere of *Hotel for Dogs*. Some people expected the dogs to howl and bark constantly, but they were very well behaved. Some dogs only howled when they heard dogs howling in the movie.

Watch out for the next dog-friendly movie!

Nikki and her Rhodesian ridgeback puppy, Sookie, at Melbourne's Moonlight Cinema

relaxing at the Moonlight Cinema

Screen Up ... Up ... Up!

The massive screen starts to move upwards.

ready to screen the movie

Dog tired!

Rules for Dog Owners ... and Dogs, Too!

Dog owners must observe these rules at the Moonlight Cinema:

Short Leash: dogs must be held on a short leash (two metres or less) by an adult.

Aggressive or Muzzled Dogs: they are not admitted to the gardens.

Aggressive During the Movie: if dogs bark, snap, snarl or bite any dog or human, the owner will be asked to remove their dog immediately.

No Chocolate or Macadamia Nuts: these are lethal for dogs to eat so these foods are prohibited and are not sold at the candy bar.

Dog Excrement: extra biodegradable bags are available at the venue. Owners must immediately clean up any dog excrement and put the tied bag into the bins.

Water: owners must bring water bowls for their dogs.

Karen, Kate and Sam with their beloved boxers, Babe and Kobi

GOLD CLASS OR GOLD GRASS?

For an extra-special cinema experience, people enjoy Gold Class. But in the gardens, movies can be watched from special "seats" in "Gold Grass".

Index

Glossary

acoustic Describes material that is soft and absorbs noise, used to improve sound quality in cinemas

architect A person who designs buildings

Art Deco A style of decoration from the 1920s and 1930s that uses bold shapes and bright colours

cinemascope Describes films projected onto a screen that is wider than it is high (but not as wide as wide-screen)

cinema shell The basic building structure that exists before an architect designs the cinema interior

platter A horizontal rotating table used to feed film to a projector

projectionist Someone who operates the projectors to show movies on the screens at a cinema

sight line An imaginary line from a person's eye to what they can see (such as the screen at a cinema)

title card Printed text that appeared on the screen during a silent movie to explain what was happening

wide-screen Describes films projected onto a screen that is extra wide in relation to its height (wider than cinemascope)